Miracles of the Bible

Light Shining Out of Darkness

God moves in a mysterious way,
　　His wonders to perform;
He plants His footsteps in the sea
　　And rides upon the storm.

Deep in unfathomable mines
　　Of never-failing skill,
He treasures His bright designs
　　And works His sovereign will.

Ye fearful faints, fresh courage take;
　　The clouds ye so much dread
Are big with mercy and shall break
　　In blessings on your head.

Judge not the Lord by feeble sense,
　　But trust Him for His grace;
Behind a frowning Providence
　　He hides a smiling face.

His purposes will ripen fast,
　　Unfolding every hour;
The bud may have a bitter taste,
　　But sweet will be the flower.

Blind unbelief is sure to err,
　　And scan His work in vain;
God is His own interpreter,
　　And He will make it plain.

–William Cowper

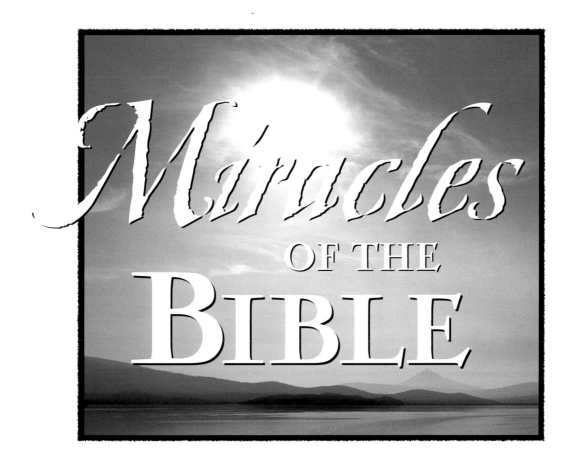

Miracles
OF THE
BIBLE

Julie K. Hogan, Editor

IDEALS PUBLICATIONS
NASHVILLE, TENNESSEE

NOTE: Debate among historians and archaeologists continues as to the precise locations of the miraculous biblical events included within. Because there are no definitive locations, the contemporary photographs in these pages are only examples of where the miracles *might* have occurred: where historians and scholars think an event may have occurred or where traditionally a site is located. This book is intended only to provide insight into the miracles of God, not to locate the miracle on Earth.

First published in this format in 2005

ISBN 0-8249-5882-9

Published by Ideals Publications
A division of Guideposts
535 Metroplex Drive, Suite 250
Nashville, Tennessee 37211
www.idealsbooks.com

Printed and bound in Italy
10 9 8 7 6 5 4 3 2 1

Copyright © 2004 by Ideals Publications

Publisher, Patricia A. Pingry
Assistant Editor, Katie Patton
Research Assistant, Mary P. Dunn

Library of Congress Cataloging-in-Publication Data

Bible. English. Selections. 2004.
  Miracles of the Bible / edited by Julie K. Hogan.
    p. cm.
            (alk. paper)
  1. Miracles—Quotations, maxims, etc. 2. Bible—Quotations.
  I. Hogan, Julie, 1949- II. Title.
  BS680.M5H63 2004
  220.6—dc22

                           2004006380

PHOTO ACKNOWLEDGMENTS

Cover (background) Dennis Frates, (inset) The Image Bank/Chuck Fishman (Getty Images); title page PowerStock/SuperStock; p. 5 (top) Alamy Images, (bottom) Israel Images/Garo Nalbandian; p. 7 Alamy Images; pp. 8-9 PowerStock/SuperStock; pp. 10-11 NASA/JPL-Caltech/S. Willner; pp. 12-13 Alamy Images; pp. 14-15 Israel Images/Hanan Isachar; pp. 16-17 John Warden/SuperStock; pp. 18-19 SuperStock; pp. 20-21 Israel Images/Hanan Isachar; p. 23 Israel Images/Steven Allan; pp. 24-25 Caroline Von Tuempling/SuperStock; pp. 26-27 Steve Vidler/SuperStock; pp. 28-29 Steve Vidler/SuperStock; pp. 30-31 SuperStock; pp. 32-33 Alamy Images; pp. 34-35 Tony Stone/Tom Till (Getty Images); pp. 36-37 Stock Image/SuperStock; pp. 38-39 The Image Bank/Toshihiko Chinami (Getty Images); pp. 40-41 Taxi/Getty Images; p. 43 Israel Images/Hanan Isachar; p. 45 Roberts Stock/Zefa; pp. 46-47 Israel Images/Hanan Isachar; pp. 48-49 Israel Images/Hanan Isachar; pp. 50-51 Tony Stone/Michel Setboun (Getty Images); p. 53 Israel Images/Shai Ginott; p. 55 Israel Images/Richard Nowitz; pp. 56-57 Israel Images/Garo Nalbandian; p. 59 Israel Images/ Doron Nisim; pp. 60-61 Israel Images/Hanan Isachar; p. 63 Israel Images/Hanan Isachar; pp. 64-65 Alamy Images; p. 67 Kurt Scholz/SuperStock; p. 69 Silvio Fiore/SuperStock; p. 71 Israel Images/Garo Nalbandian; pp. 72-73 Israel Images/Shai Ginott; pp. 74-75 Tony Stone/Denis Waugh (Getty Images); p. 77 Steve Vidler/SuperStock; p. 79 Israel Images/Hanan Isachar; p. 81 Israel Images/Israel Talby; pp. 82-83 Israel Images/Hanan Isachar; pp. 84-85 Israel Images/Hanan Isachar; pp. 86-87 The Image Bank/Chuck Fishman (Getty Images); pp. 88-89 Israel Images/Israel Talby; pp. 90-91 Israel Images/Tsur Pelly; pp. 92-93 Israel Images/Garo Nalbandian; pp. 94-95 Israel Images/Israel Talby; p. 97 Israel Images/Hanan Isachar; p. 99 Israel Images/Richard Nowitz; pp. 100-101 Israel Images/G. Geffen; p. 103 Roberts Stock/R. Kord; p. 105 Israel Images/Richard Nowitz; p. 107 Israel Images/Hanan Isachar; p. 108 Alamy Images; pp. 110-111 SEF/Art Resource, NY; pp. 112-113 Israel Images/Hanan Isachar; pp. 114-115 Roberts Stock/R. Kord; p. 117 Israel Images/Hanan Isachar; pp. 118-119 Israel Images/Hanan Isachar *(continued on p. 160)*

Contents

Miracles of the

The Old Testament is filled with examples of God's miraculous intervention—from the creation of the universe itself to the parting of the Red Sea to the provision of manna in the wilderness. Each event exemplifies God's limitless power, his sovereignty over all creation, and his unequaled love and compassion for mankind.

In the following pages are biblical passages that tell of some of these miracles along with contemporary photographs of the places where the miracles are thought to have taken place.

Old Testament

Chapter ONE

MIRACLES OF CREATION

Let There Be Light

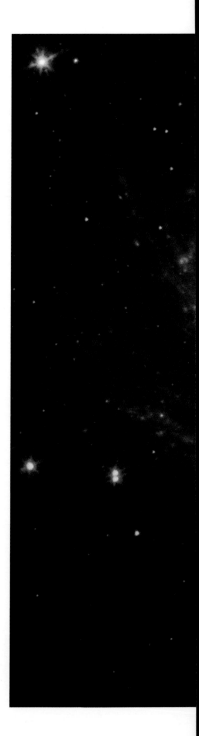

*I*n the beginning God created the heaven and the earth. And the earth was without form, and void; and darkness was upon the face of the deep. And the Spirit of God moved upon the face of the waters. And God said, Let there be light: and there was light.

The first recorded miracle in the Bible takes place in the heavens, in the vast reaches of unformed space where there was only darkness and nothing else. Opposite is a photograph from a NASA telescope showing a galaxy much like our Milky Way. This photograph gives us just a tiny glimpse of the magnitude of God.

Heaven and Earth

GENESIS 1:4–6, 8–10

And God divided the light from the darkness. And God called the light Day, and the darkness he called Night. . . . And God said, Let there be a firmament in the midst of the waters, and let it divide the waters from the waters. And God called the firmament Heaven. And God said, Let the waters under the heaven be gathered together unto one place, and let the dry land appear: and it was so. And God called the dry land Earth; . . . and God saw that it was good.

This photograph of our planet Earth was taken from millions of miles away. Seen from this perspective, we can only stare in awe at the magnificence of the miracle of the creation of Earth.

God Creates Plants

And God said, Let the
earth bring forth grass,
the herb yielding seed, and the fruit
tree yielding fruit after his kind . . .
and it was so. And the earth brought
forth grass, and herb yielding seed
after his kind, and the tree yielding
fruit . . . and God saw that it
was good.

The miracle of creation continued with the creation
of plants, like those seen in this photograph of
brilliant red and yellow poppies with pine trees in
the distance at the Ben Shemen Forest in the
Shephelah region of Israel.

Fish and Flying Things

GENESIS 1:20-21

And God said, Let the waters bring forth abundantly the moving creature that hath life, and fowl that may fly above the earth in the open firmament of heaven. And God created great whales, and every living creature that moveth, which the waters brought forth abundantly, after their kind, and every winged fowl after his kind: and God saw that it was good.

The leaping humpback whale, in the icy waters of Alaska, shows the beauty, grace, and magnitude of God's creation of sea creatures and flying fowl on the fifth day.

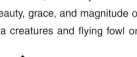

God Creates Animals

GENESIS 1:24-25

And God said, Let the earth bring forth the living creature after his kind, cattle, and creeping thing, and beast of the earth after his kind: and it was so.

And God made the beast of the earth after his kind, and cattle after their kind, and every thing that creepeth upon the earth after his kind: and God saw that it was good.

On the sixth day of Creation, God made all the land animals, from the roaring lion to the lowly lamb. This mother giraffe and her baby, on the African plain, exhibit God's handiwork in their graceful necks and unique spots.

Chapter Two

MIRACLES OF THE EXODUS

The Burning Bush

EXODUS 3:2–10

The angel of the LORD appeared unto [Moses] in a flame of fire out of the midst of a bush: and he looked, and, behold, the bush burned with fire, and the bush was not consumed. . . . God called unto him out of the midst of the bush, and said, Moses, Moses . . . I am come down to deliver [the Israelites] out of the hand of the Egyptians, and to bring them up out of that land unto a good land and a large, unto a land flowing with milk and honey. . . . I will send thee unto Pharaoh, that thou mayest bring forth my people the children of Israel out of Egypt.

Pictured here is the type of bush that many believe "burned but was not consumed." The plant is a rare mountain thornbush similar to the raspberry bush. The bush shown here grows beside the chapel at Saint Catherine's Monastery on the Mount of God in the Sinai Desert. Some people believe this is the actual burning bush through which God spoke to Moses more than three thousand years ago.

Aaron's Rod

EXODUS 7:10–14

Moses and Aaron went in unto Pharaoh, and they did so as the LORD had commanded: and Aaron cast down his rod before Pharaoh, and before his servants, and it became a serpent. Then Pharaoh also called the wise men and the sorcerers: now the magicians of Egypt, they also did in like manner with their enchantments. For they cast down every man his rod, and they became serpents: but Aaron's rod swallowed up their rods. . . . And the LORD said unto Moses, Pharaoh's heart is hardened, he refuseth to let the people go.

The Great Pyramids of Giza in Egypt, where God first displayed his miracles before the Pharaoh, were massive monuments constructed above the tombs of kings. The largest of the pyramids is one of the Seven Wonders of the Ancient World and covers thirteen acres. Some of its blocks are estimated to weigh more than sixty tons.

The River Turns to Blood

EXODUS 7:20–21

*A*nd Moses and Aaron . . . did as the LORD commanded; and he lifted up the rod, and smote the waters that were in the river, in the sight of Pharaoh, and in the sight of his servants; and all the waters that were in the river were turned to blood. And the fish that was in the river died; and the river stank, and the Egyptians could not drink of the water of the river.

The 3,500 mile-long Nile River was essential to Egypt's prosperity in Moses' day. The great river would flood annually, enriching the dry land around it. The Nile was personified by the Egyptians as a god and worshiped through religious celebrations and offerings. It was a principal means of transportation, supported a fishing industry, and provided the papyrus reeds that were used to make paper, baskets, and sails for Egyptian boats. The boats in the picture are called *feluccas*, and are a common sight on the Nile today.

The Tenth Plague

E X O D U S   1 2 : 2 9 – 3 1

And it came to pass, that at midnight the LORD smote all the firstborn in the land of Egypt, from the firstborn of Pharaoh that sat on his throne unto the firstborn of the captive that was in the dungeon. . . . and there was a great cry in Egypt; for there was not a house where there was not one dead. And he called for Moses and Aaron by night, and said, Rise up, and get you forth from among my people, both ye and the children of Israel; and go, serve the LORD, as ye have said.

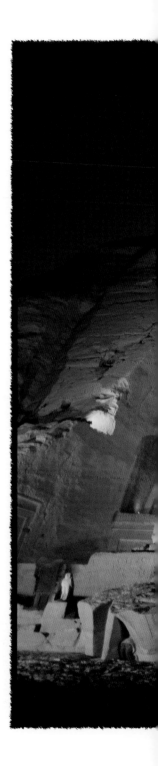

The exact date of the Hebrews' Exodus from Eygpt is unknown, though some believe Ramses II was Pharaoh during the time of the Exodus. Often called Ramses "the Great," he was one of the greatest builders in Egypt's history, erecting massive monuments to himself in every Egyptian city. The photograph opposite is one example of these monuments built in Abu Simbel, Egypt, fronted by the massive statues of Ramses II.

Pillar of
Cloud and Fire

EXODUS 13:17–18, 20–22

And it came to pass, when Pharaoh had let the people go, that . . . God led the people about. And they took their journey from Succoth, and encamped in Etham, in the edge of the wilderness. And the LORD went before them by day in a pillar of a cloud, to lead them the way; and by night in a pillar of fire, to give them light; to go by day and night: He took not away the pillar of the cloud by day, nor the pillar of fire by night, from before the people.

The wilderness through which the Israelites traveled for forty years is what is now called the Sinai Peninsula, in present-day Egypt. The peninsula's landscape is an area of many contrasts. A plateau slopes down to the Mediterranean Sea on the north, and toward the south is a series of rugged mountains. Wasteland comprises much of the landscape in between. The photo at right shows the rocky formations and strange pathways that often lead through Egypt's Sinai Peninsula.

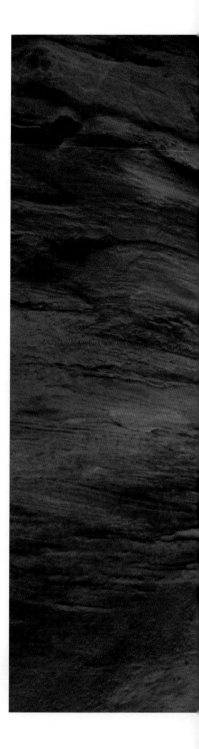

Parting of the Red Sea

EXODUS 14:21–22, 30

And Moses stretched out his hand over the sea; and the LORD caused the sea to go back by a strong east wind all that night, and made the sea dry land, and the waters were divided. And the children of Israel went into the midst of the sea upon the dry ground: and the waters were a wall unto them on their right hand, and on their left. . . . Thus the LORD saved Israel that day out of the hand of the Egyptians.

The Red Sea, seen in this photograph taken off the shore of Egypt, stretches for almost 1,300 miles. It is usually a bright blue, but it receives its name from the algae that often grows in the water, causing the sea to look reddish-brown. The Red Sea is one of the hottest and saltiest bodies of water on earth. At its northern end, the Red Sea touches the Sinai Peninsula, where it then branches into two canals. Some think the Israelites may have crossed one of these bodies of water.

Chapter THREE

MIRACLES
IN THE
WILDERNESS

Bitter Water Made Sweet

EXODUS 15:22–25

So Moses brought Israel from the Red Sea, and they went out into the wilderness of Shur; and they went three days in the wilderness, and found no water. And when they came to Marah, they could not drink of the waters of Marah, for they were bitter: therefore the name of it was called Marah. And the people murmured against Moses, saying, What shall we drink? And he cried unto the LORD; and the LORD shewed him a tree, which when he had cast into the waters, the waters were made sweet: there he made for them a statute and an ordinance, and there he proved them.

After the Israelites crossed the Red Sea, they came to the wilderness of Shur, which was located at the northwestern region of the Sinai Peninsula, in what is part of Egypt today. The fertile land of Egypt was watered by the Nile River and was often covered in rich vegetation, as shown in the picture at right. The Sinai Peninsula is not entirely a desert region itself and supports streams and plant life in the midst of its rocky terrain.

Food in the Wilderness

EXODUS 16:11–14, 31, 35

And the LORD spake unto Moses, saying, I have heard the murmurings of the children of Israel: speak unto them, saying, At even ye shall eat flesh, and in the morning ye shall be filled with bread; and ye shall know that I am the LORD your God. And it came to pass, that at even the quails came up, and covered the camp: and in the morning the dew lay round about the host. And when the dew that lay was gone up, behold, upon the face of the wilderness there lay a small round thing, as small as the hoar frost on the ground . . . and the taste of it was like wafers made with honey. And the children of Israel did eat manna forty years . . . until they came unto the borders of the land of Canaan.

The picture at right shows the rugged terrain of the Sinai Peninsula, where God's manna fed the Israelites. Many of the places in which the Israelites encamped while traveling through the wilderness cannot be exactly identified. Though Sinai was called a wilderness, it was not a desert. Water could still be found in small streams and the occasional oasis, and there would have been enough grassland for animals to graze.

The Ten Commandments

EXODUS 24:12, 15–18; 31:18

And the LORD said unto Moses, Come up to me into the mount, and be there: and I will give thee tables of stone, and a law, and commandments which I have written; that thou mayest teach them. And Moses went up into the mount, and a cloud covered the mount. And the glory of the LORD abode upon mount Sinai, and the cloud covered it six days: and the seventh day he called unto Moses out of the midst of the cloud. And the sight of the glory of the LORD was like devouring fire on the top of the mount in the eyes of the children of Israel. And Moses went into the midst of the cloud, and gat him up into the mount: and Moses was in the mount forty days and forty nights. And [the LORD] gave unto Moses, when he had made an end of communing with him upon mount Sinai, two tables of testimony, tables of stone, written with the finger of God.

Jebel Musa, seen here from its base, means "Moses' Mountain," and it is the peak on the southern Sinai Peninsula thought to be the Mount Sinai of the Bible, where Moses received God's commandments. Jebel Musa is one of a cluster of three peaks and has a broad plain at its base, where the Israelites may have camped. It is also called Mount Horeb in the Bible.

God Parts the Jordan River

JOSHUA 3:14–17

And it came to pass, when the people removed from their tents, to pass over Jordan, and the priests bearing the ark of the covenant before the people; And as they that bare the ark were come unto Jordan, and the feet of the priests that bare the ark were dipped in the brim of the water, (for Jordan overfloweth all his banks all the time of harvest,) That the waters which came down from above stood and rose up upon an heap very far from the city Adam, that is beside Zaretan: and those that came down toward the sea of the plain, even the salt sea, failed, and were cut off: and the people passed over right against Jericho. And the priests that bare the ark of the covenant of the LORD stood firm on dry ground in the midst of Jordan, and all the Israelites passed over on dry ground, until all the people were passed clean over Jordan.

The Jordan is Israel's longest and most important river. It runs north-south starting from the Sea of Galilee and is situated in a valley that descends dramatically into the Dead Sea, where the river ends. The river can be forded in a few places, but for the most part it is too deep to cross. The Israelites under Joshua crossed at the south end of the river, near Jericho. They crossed from the east, entering the Promised Land for the first time.

The Walls of Jericho

JOSHUA 6:2-5, 15-16, 20

The LORD said unto Joshua, See, I have given into thine hand Jericho, and the king thereof, and the mighty men of valour. And ye shall compass the city. . . . And it shall come to pass, that when they make a long blast with the ram's horn, and when ye hear the sound of the trumpet, all the people shall shout with a great shout; and the wall of the city shall fall down flat, and the people shall ascend up every man straight before him. And it came to pass on the seventh day, that they rose early about the dawning of the day, and compassed the city after the same manner seven times: only on that day they compassed the city seven times. And it came to pass at the seventh time, when the priests blew with the trumpets, Joshua said unto the people, Shout; for the LORD hath given you the city. So the people shouted when the priests blew with the trumpets: and it came to pass, when the people heard the sound of the trumpet, and the people shouted with a great shout, that the wall fell down flat, so that the people went up into the city, every man straight before him, and they took the city.

The city of Jericho is one of the oldest cities in the world. It was already an ancient city in Joshua's day, surrounded by thick walls on which guards could be stationed. When they attacked the city, the Israelite priests each carried a ram's horn, or *shofar*, as shown in the photo opposite of a modern-day Jew in traditional dress, blowing the shofar at Jerusalem's Wailing Wall. These trumpets were used normally to announce feasts or to signal a call to battle—but God commanded that they be used to bring down the walls of the ancient city of Jericho.

The Sun Stands Still

JOSHUA 10:6, 8–14

And the men of Gibeon sent unto Joshua to the camp to Gilgal, saying, Slack not thy hand from thy servants; come up to us quickly, and save us, and help us: for all the kings of the Amorites that dwell in the mountains are gathered together against us. . . . The LORD said unto Joshua, Fear them not: for I have delivered them into thine hand; there shall not a man of them stand before thee. Joshua therefore came unto them suddenly, and went up from Gilgal all night. And the LORD discomfited them before Israel, and slew them with a great slaughter at Gibeon. . . . And it came to pass, as they fled from before Israel, and were in the going down to Bethhoron, that the LORD cast down great stones from heaven upon them unto Azekah, and they died: they were more which died with hailstones than they whom the children of Israel slew with the sword. Then spake Joshua to the LORD in the day when the LORD delivered up the Amorites before the children of Israel, and he said in the sight of Israel, Sun, stand thou still upon Gibeon; and thou, Moon, in the valley of Ajalon. . . . So the sun stood still in the midst of heaven, and hasted not to go down about a whole day. And there was no day like that before it or after it, that the LORD hearkened unto the voice of a man: for the LORD fought for Israel.

The book of Joshua tells us of the amazing incident where "the Lord hearkened unto the voice of a man" when God did not allow the sun to set nor the moon to go down over the valley of Ajalon. In the photograph above is the present-day Ayalon Valley, located approximately fifteen miles northwest of Jerusalem.

Chapter FOUR

MIRACLES
OF THE
PROPHETS

The Ravens Feed Elijah

I KINGS 17:2–6

And the word of the LORD came unto [Elijah the Tishbite], saying, Get thee hence, and turn thee eastward, and hide thyself by the brook Cherith, that is before Jordan. And it shall be, that thou shalt drink of the brook; and I have commanded the ravens to feed thee there. So he went and did according unto the word of the LORD: for he went and dwelt by the brook Cherith, that is before Jordan. And the ravens brought him bread and flesh in the morning, and bread and flesh in the evening; and he drank of the brook.

The location of the river Cherith, where God sheltered Elijah and fed him by the ravens, is debated. One traditionally recognized location is a few miles south of Jericho in the Judean desert, as shown here. Today the gorge is called Wadi el Qelt. A wadi is a riverbed that usually remains dry except during the rainy season, when a stream flows through the parched ravine.

Oil and Meal Renewed

I KINGS 17:7–16

And the word of the LORD came unto [Elijah], saying, Arise, get thee to Zarephath, which belongeth to Zidon, and dwell there: behold, I have commanded a widow woman there to sustain thee. So he arose and went to Zarephath. And when he came to the gate of the city, behold, the widow woman was there gathering of sticks: and he called to her, and said, Fetch me, I pray thee, a little water in a vessel, that I may drink. And as she was going to fetch it, he called to her, and said, Bring me, I pray thee, a morsel of bread in thine hand. And she said, As the LORD thy God liveth, I have not a cake, but an handful of meal in a barrel, and a little oil in a cruse: and, behold, I am gathering two sticks, that I may go in and dress it for me and my son, that we may eat it, and die. And Elijah said unto her, Fear not; go and do as thou hast said: but make me thereof a little cake first, and bring it unto me, and after make for thee and for thy son. For thus saith the LORD God of Israel, The barrel of meal shall not waste, neither shall the cruse of oil fail, until the day that the LORD sendeth rain upon the earth. And she went and did according to the saying of Elijah: and she, and he, and her house, did eat many days. And the barrel of meal wasted not, neither did the cruse of oil fail, according to the word of the LORD, which he spake by Elijah.

The picture at right gives a glimpse into life in Old Testament time. The small millstone on the left was used to grind grain into flour. A fire would be started inside the rounded oven, and the dough would be spread on the outside of the oven to be baked into bread.

The Widow's Son

I KINGS 17:17–24

And it came to pass after these things, that the son of the woman, the mistress of the house, fell sick; and his sickness was so sore, that there was no breath left in him. And she said unto Elijah, What have I to do with thee, O thou man of God? art thou come unto me to call my sin to remembrance, and to slay my son? And he said unto her, Give me thy son. And he took him out of her bosom, and carried him up into a loft, where he abode, and laid him upon his own bed. And he cried unto the LORD, and said, O LORD my God, hast thou also brought evil upon the widow with whom I sojourn, by slaying her son? And he stretched himself upon the child three times, and cried unto the LORD, and said, O LORD my God, I pray thee, let this child's soul come into him again. And the LORD heard the voice of Elijah; and the soul of the child came into him again, and he revived. And Elijah took the child, and brought him down out of the chamber into the house, and delivered him unto his mother: and Elijah said, See, thy son liveth. And the woman said to Elijah, Now by this I know that thou art a man of God, and that the word of the LORD in thy mouth is truth.

In biblical times, houses were built with flat roofs, with a staircase on the outside leading up to the roof. This extra space provided room for washing clothes, drying fruits and grains, and enjoying the cool breezes on dry, hot nights. Spare rooftop rooms were often built to accommodate guests. The photo at right shows a stone doorway leading up to the roof in an ancient Palestinian house.

God Sends Rain

I KINGS 18:41–46

And Elijah said unto Ahab, Get thee up, eat and drink; for there is a sound of abundance of rain. So Ahab went up to eat and to drink. And Elijah went up to the top of Carmel; and he cast himself down upon the earth, and put his face between his knees, And said to his servant, Go up now, look toward the sea. And he went up, and looked, and said, There is nothing. And he said, Go again seven times. And it came to pass at the seventh time, that he said, Behold, there ariseth a little cloud out of the sea, like a man's hand. And he said, Go up, say unto Ahab, Prepare thy chariot, and get thee down that the rain stop thee not. And it came to pass in the mean while, that the heaven was black with clouds and wind, and there was a great rain. And Ahab rode, and went to Jezreel. And the hand of the LORD was on Elijah; and he girded up his loins, and ran before Ahab to the entrance of Jezreel.

Mount Carmel, located near the Mediterranean Sea, is the place from which Elijah saw the cloud that foretold the coming of the long-awaited rains. This area of the Middle East becomes very hot and dry during the summer, when little rain falls. Winter rains prevent the land from becoming a desert. This picture shows storm clouds rolling in across the Hinnom Valley near Jerusalem.

Elijah Taken Up to Heaven

II KINGS 2:1–2, 8–11

And it came to pass, when the LORD would take up Elijah into heaven by a whirlwind, that Elijah went with Elisha from Gilgal. And Elijah said unto Elisha, Tarry here, I pray thee; for the LORD hath sent me to Bethel. And Elisha said unto him, As the LORD liveth, and as thy soul liveth, I will not leave thee. So they went down to Bethel. And Elijah took his mantle, and wrapped it together, and smote the waters, and they were divided hither and thither, so that they two went over on dry ground. And it came to pass, when they were gone over, that Elijah said unto Elisha, Ask what I shall do for thee, before I be taken away from thee. And Elisha said, I pray thee, let a double portion of thy spirit be upon me. And he said, Thou hast asked a hard thing: nevertheless, if thou see me when I am taken from thee, it shall be so unto thee; but if not, it shall not be so. And it came to pass, as they still went on, and talked, that, behold, there appeared a chariot of fire, and horses of fire, and parted them both asunder; and Elijah went up by a whirlwind into heaven.

God performed a miracle through Elijah as one of the last events in his life, when Elijah parted the waters of the Jordan River and then was taken up in "a chariot of fire." Whirlwinds are quite common in Judea, where desert lands are in proximity to cooler bodies of water. The whirlwind at right was photographed in the Negev Desert of southern Israel.

The Widow's Oil

II Kings 4:1-7

Now there cried a certain woman of the wives of the sons of the prophets unto Elisha, saying, Thy servant my husband is dead; and thou knowest that thy servant did fear the LORD: and the creditor is come to take unto him my two sons to be bondmen. And Elisha said unto her . . . Go, borrow thee vessels abroad of all thy neighbours, even empty vessels; borrow not a few. And when thou art come in, thou shalt shut the door upon thee and upon thy sons, and shalt pour out into all those vessels, and thou shalt set aside that which is full. So she went from him, and shut the door upon her and upon her sons, who brought the vessels to her; and she poured out. And it came to pass, when the vessels were full, that she said unto her son, Bring me yet a vessel. And he said unto her, There is not a vessel more. And the oil stayed. Then she came and told the man of God. And he said, Go, sell the oil, and pay thy debt, and live thou and thy children of the rest.

In the time of Elisha, oil was used as fuel for lamps, for anointing, for cooking, and for dressing wounds. It was a valuable commodity in commerce. The oil the widow used was probably that made from green olives, which grow in abundance in Israel. Olive trees, which grow slowly and can produce fruit for many years, were cultivated in groves, such as the one shown here near modern-day Jerusalem.

The Shunammite Boy

II KINGS 4:18–21, 32–35

And when the child was grown, it fell on a day, that he went out to his father to the reapers. And he said unto his father, My head, my head. And he said to a lad, Carry him to his mother. And when he had taken him, and brought him to his mother, he sat on her knees till noon, and then died. And she went up, and laid him on the bed of the man of God, and shut the door upon him. So she went and came unto the man of God to Mount Carmel. And when Elisha was come into the house, behold, the child was dead, and laid upon his bed. He went in therefore, and shut the door upon them twain, and prayed unto the LORD. And he went up, and lay upon the child, and put his mouth upon his mouth, and his eyes upon his eyes, and his hands upon his hands: and he stretched himself upon the child; and the flesh of the child waxed warm. Then he returned, and walked in the house to and fro; and went up, and stretched himself upon him: and the child sneezed seven times, and the child opened his eyes.

The town of Shunem, present-day Sulam, was a border city in northern Israel, located in the Jezreel Valley near Mount Gilboa. The Jezreel Valley separates Samaria from Galilee, and it was the major passageway through the rugged Judean hills. Many historic battles took place in this valley, and the Greek word for the area is Armageddon. The Jezreel Valley is shown here, as it is today.

Naaman

II KINGS 5:1, 9–14

So Naaman [a leper] came with his horses and with his chariot, and stood at the door of the house of Elisha. And Elisha sent a messenger unto him, saying, Go and wash in Jordan seven times, and thy flesh shall come again to thee, and thou shalt be clean. But Naaman was wroth, and went away, and said, Behold, I thought, He will surely come out to me, and stand, and call on the name of the LORD his God, and strike his hand over the place, and recover the leper. Are not Abana and Pharpar, rivers of Damascus, better than all the waters of Israel? may I not wash in them, and be clean? . . . And his servants came near, and spake unto him, and said, My father, if the prophet had bid thee do some great thing, wouldest thou not have done it? how much rather then, when he saith to thee, Wash, and be clean? Then went he down, and dipped himself seven times in Jordan, according to the saying of the man of God: and his flesh came again like unto the flesh of a little child, and he was clean.

The Jordan River makes a natural boundary between present-day Israel and Jordan. With its winding course, it is not easily navigated. The northern section of the river has many tributaries that provide for fertile farmland, and the southern end is surrounded by dry desert with an occasional oasis. The photo at right shows the lower Jordan River as it winds peacefully through Judea.

Shadrach, Meshach, and Abednego

DANIEL 3:19–20, 22–28

hen was Nebuchadnezzar full of fury . . . and commanded that
they should heat the furnace one seven times more than it was
wont to be heated. And he commanded the most mighty men that were
in his army to bind Shadrach, Meshach, and Abednego, and to cast
them into the burning fiery furnace. Therefore because the king's
commandment was urgent, and the furnace exceeding hot, the flames
of the fire slew those men that took up Shadrach, Meshach, and
Abednego. And these three men, Shadrach, Meshach, and Abednego,
fell down bound into the midst of the burning fiery furnace. Then
Nebuchadnezzar the king was astonished . . . and said, Lo, I see four
men loose, walking in the midst of the fire, and they have no hurt; and
the form of the fourth is like the Son of God. Then Nebuchadnezzar
came near to the mouth of the burning fiery furnace, and spake, and
said, Shadrach, Meshach, and Abednego, ye servants of the most high
God, come forth, and come hither. Then Shadrach, Meshach, and
Abednego, came forth of the midst of the fire . . . upon whose bodies
the fire had no power, nor was an hair of their head singed, neither were
their coats changed, nor the smell of fire had passed on them. Then
Nebuchadnezzar spake, and said, Blessed be the God of Shadrach,
Meshach, and Abednego, who hath sent his angel, and delivered his
servants that trusted in him!

The city of Babylon, where the Jews were exiled under Nebuchadnezzar, is over 4,300 years old, making it one of the oldest cities in the world. Excavations have uncovered the ruins of the ancient city fifty miles south of the modern city of Baghdad in Iraq. There the great Ishtar Gate has been reconstructed, as shown above. The gate led through the massive double walls that surrounded the city, and was decorated with the *sirrush*, the mythical dragon of the Babylonian god Marduk.

Daniel and the Lion's Den

DANIEL 6:16–17, 19–23, 25–27

Then the king [Darius] commanded, and they brought Daniel, and cast him into the den of lions. Now the king spake and said unto Daniel, Thy God whom thou servest continually, he will deliver thee. And a stone was brought, and laid upon the mouth of the den; and the king sealed it with his own signet, and with the signet of his lords; that the purpose might not be changed concerning Daniel. Then the king arose very early in the morning, and went in haste unto the den of lions. . . . and the king spake and said to Daniel, O Daniel, servant of the living God, is thy God, whom thou servest continually, able to deliver thee from the lions? Then said Daniel unto the king, O king, live for ever. My God hath sent his angel, and hath shut the lions' mouths, that they have not hurt me: forasmuch as before him innocency was found in me; and also before thee, O king, have I done no hurt. Then was the king exceedingly glad for him, and commanded that they should take Daniel up out of the den. So Daniel was taken up out of the den, and no manner of hurt was found upon him, because he believed in his God. Then king Darius wrote unto all people, . . . I make a decree, That in every dominion of my kingdom men tremble and fear before the God of Daniel: for he is the living God, and stedfast for ever, and his kingdom that which shall not be destroyed, and his dominion shall be even unto the end.

Both the Persian king Cyrus and his grandson Darius I are buried in elaborate tombs in Persepolis, the ancient capital of the Persian Empire, located in modern-day Iran. The ruins at right are the remains of Darius's Palace, burned by Alexander the Great when he conquered Persia.

Miracles of the

Like the Old Testament, the New

Testament recounts numerous examples of God's miraculous intervention. Most of the New Testament miracles were performed by Jesus, some by his disciples. From the changing of the water into wine to the feeding of the multitude to Paul's healing of the sick, each event illustrates once again God's endless power and his love for mankind—none more so than the ultimate miracle of Jesus' resurrection.

In the following pages are biblical passages that tell of some of these miracles along with contemporary photographs of the places where the miracles are thought to have taken place.

New Testament

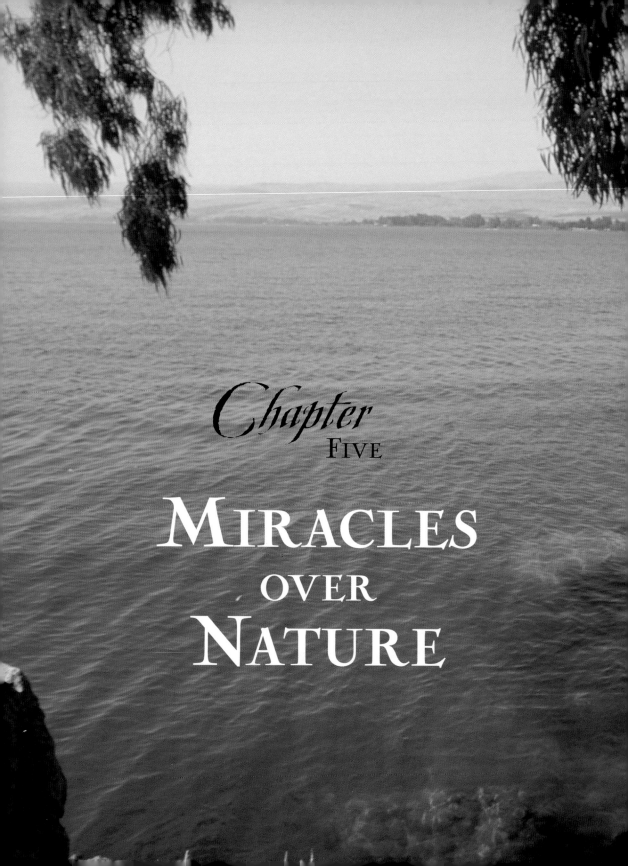

Chapter Five

Miracles over Nature

Angels Proclaim Jesus' Birth

LUKE 2:8–14

And there were in the same country shepherds abiding in the field, keeping watch over their flock by night. And, lo, the angel of the Lord came upon them, and the glory of the Lord shone round about them: and they were sore afraid. And the angel said unto them, Fear not: for, behold, I bring you good tidings of great joy, which shall be to all people. For unto you is born this day in the city of David a Saviour, which is Christ the Lord. And this shall be a sign unto you; Ye shall find the babe wrapped in swaddling clothes, lying in a manger. And suddenly there was with the angel a multitude of the heavenly host praising God, and saying, Glory to God in the highest, and on earth peace, good will toward men.

Though small and seemingly insignificant, the little town of Bethlehem, situated about five miles south of Jerusalem, holds a place of honor in Israel's history. The countryside shown in the photo opposite is the place where the lowly shepherds received from the angels the news of Jesus' birth.

The Star of Bethlehem

MATTHEW 2:1–9

Now when Jesus was born in Bethlehem of Judaea in the days of Herod the king, behold, there came wise men from the east to Jerusalem, Saying, Where is he that is born King of the Jews? for we have seen his star in the east, and are come to worship him. When Herod the king had heard these things, he . . . gathered all the chief priests and scribes of the people together, he demanded of them where Christ should be born. And they said unto him, In Bethlehem of Judaea: for thus it is written by the prophet, And thou Bethlehem, in the land of Judah, art not the least among the princes of Judah: for out of thee shall come a Governor, that shall rule my people Israel. Then Herod, when he had privily called the wise men, inquired of them diligently what time the star appeared. And he sent them to Bethlehem. . . . When they had heard the king, they departed; and, lo, the star, which they saw in the east, went before them, till it came and stood over where the young child was.

God provided a star as a guide for the wise men who followed it until "it stood over where the young child was." The wise men, or Magi, came from the east and were possibly Persian astrologers who recognized the star of Bethlehem as a sign from God. The Magi most likely traveled by camel, sturdy animals well-suited to long desert journeys. Camels, like that shown here, are still used in the Middle East as a means of transportation.

The Wedding at Cana

JOHN 2:1–11

And the third day there was a marriage in Cana of Galilee; and the mother of Jesus was there. . . . And when they wanted wine, the mother of Jesus saith unto him, They have no wine. Jesus saith unto her, Woman, what have I to do with thee? mine hour is not yet come. His mother saith unto the servants, Whatsoever he saith unto you, do it. . . . Jesus saith unto them, Fill the waterpots with water. And they filled them up to the brim. And he saith unto them, Draw out now, and bear unto the governor of the feast. And they bare it. When the ruler of the feast had tasted the water that was made wine, and knew not whence it was: (but the servants which drew the water knew;) the governor of the feast called the bridegroom, And saith unto him, Every man at the beginning doth set forth good wine; and when men have well drunk, then that which is worse: but thou hast kept the good wine until now. This beginning of miracles did Jesus in Cana of Galilee, and manifested forth his glory; and his disciples believed on him.

Although the location of Cana is debated, the town of Kafr Kana, near Jesus' hometown of Nazareth, is traditionally recognized as its site. The church at right is in Kafr Kana and is called the Wedding Church. In New Testament times, the bridegroom, accompanied by his friends, would come to the house of the bride's parents, where the wedding would take place. The whole party, and most of the community, would form a procession back to the groom's house, where the feasting and celebration would continue for seven days.

A Netful of Fish

LUKE 5:1–11

And it came to pass, that, as the people pressed upon him to hear the word of God, he stood by the lake of Gennesaret, And saw two ships standing by the lake: but the fishermen were gone out of them, and were washing their nets. And he entered into one of the ships, which was Simon's, and prayed him that he would thrust out a little from the land. And he sat down, and taught the people out of the ship. Now when he had left speaking, he said unto Simon, Launch out into the deep, and let down your nets for a draught. And Simon answering said unto him, Master, we have toiled all the night, and have taken nothing: nevertheless at thy word I will let down the net. And when they had this done, they inclosed a great multitude of fishes: and their net brake. And they beckoned unto their partners, which were in the other ship, that they should come and help them. And they came, and filled both the ships, so that they began to sink. When Simon Peter saw it, he fell down at Jesus' knees, saying, Depart from me; for I am a sinful man, O Lord. For he was astonished, and all that were with him, at the draught of the fishes which they had taken: And so was also James, and John, the sons of Zebedee, which were partners with Simon. And Jesus said unto Simon, Fear not; from henceforth thou shalt catch men. And when they had brought their ships to land, they forsook all, and followed him.

Seven of Jesus' disciples were fishermen on the Sea of Galilee, also called the Lake of Gennesaret. At the time of Jesus, there were approximately thirty fishing villages clinging to the shore of the Sea of Galilee. Most fishermen threw out small casting nets which could be handled by one man, as in this photograph of a present-day fisherman on Lake Gennesaret. For bigger catches, larger nets dragged by boats were needed. These nets were either unloaded in the boats or dragged to shore for the fish to be sorted.

Jesus Calms the Storm

MARK 4:35-41

And the same day, when the even was come, he saith unto them, Let us pass over unto the other side. And when they had sent away the multitude, they took him even as he was in the ship. And there were also with him other little ships. And there arose a great storm of wind, and the waves beat into the ship, so that it was now full. And he was in the hinder part of the ship, asleep on a pillow: and they awake him, and say unto him, Master, carest thou not that we perish? And he arose, and rebuked the wind, and said unto the sea, Peace, be still. And the wind ceased, and there was a great calm. And he said unto them, Why are ye so fearful? how is it that ye have no faith? And they feared exceedingly, and said one to another, What manner of man is this, that even the wind and the sea obey him?

Often posing peril to fishermen and boaters, the Sea of Galilee is well-known for its sudden and violent storms, as in this photo of the lake with a storm imminent. Nestled among the hills of Galilee and 680 feet below sea level, the lake is often buffeted by the force of the cool winds that rush down the mountains and stir up the warm water below, causing massive waves on the surface of the lake.

The Loaves and Fishes

JOHN 6:5–14

When Jesus then lifted up his eyes, and saw a great company come unto him, he saith unto Philip, Whence shall we buy bread, that these may eat? And this he said to prove him: for he himself knew what he would do. . . . One of his disciples, Andrew, Simon Peter's brother, saith unto him, There is a lad here, which hath five barley loaves, and two small fishes: but what are they among so many? And Jesus said, Make the men sit down. Now there was much grass in the place. So the men sat down, in number about five thousand. And Jesus took the loaves; and when he had given thanks, he distributed to the disciples, and the disciples to them that were set down; and likewise of the fishes as much as they would. When they were filled, he said unto his disciples, Gather up the fragments that remain, that nothing be lost. Therefore they gathered them together, and filled twelve baskets with the fragments of the five barley loaves, which remained over and above unto them that had eaten. Then those men, when they had seen the miracle that Jesus did, said, This is of a truth that prophet that should come into the world.

No one is quite sure where the miraculous feeding of the five thousand took place. Some say this event occured at modern-day Tabgha on the western shore of the Sea of Galilee; others say that Jesus had gone to the town of Bethsaida on the lake's eastern shore. The grassy hill shown here is the Mount of Beatitudes, near Tabgha.

Jesus Walks on Water

MATTHEW 14:24–33

But the ship was now in the midst of the sea, tossed with waves: for the wind was contrary. And in the fourth watch of the night Jesus went unto them, walking on the sea. And when the disciples saw him walking on the sea, they were troubled, saying, It is a spirit; and they cried out for fear. But straightway Jesus spake unto them, saying, Be of good cheer; it is I; be not afraid. And Peter answered him and said, Lord, if it be thou, bid me come unto thee on the water. And he said, Come. And when Peter was come down out of the ship, he walked on the water, to go to Jesus. But when he saw the wind boisterous, he was afraid; and beginning to sink, he cried, saying, Lord, save me. And immediately Jesus stretched forth his hand, and caught him, and said unto him, O thou of little faith, wherefore didst thou doubt? And when they were come into the ship, the wind ceased. Then they that were in the ship came and worshipped him, saying, Of a truth thou art the Son of God.

The Sea of Galilee is really a large lake, thirteen miles long and eight miles wide, about sixty miles north of Jerusalem. It has several names in the Bible, including the familiar Sea of Galilee: the Sea of Chinnereth, meaning "harp-shaped," for the general outline of the lake; the Lake of Gennesaret, for the fertile plain of that name lying to the northwest; and the Sea of Tiberias, for its association with the capital city of the province under Herod Antipas. The Jordan River runs through it on its passage south to the Dead Sea. When the disciples saw their Lord coming out to them on the water, it was after three o'clock in the morning—the fourth watch of the night in the Roman reckoning.

The Transfiguration

MATTHEW 17:1–8

After six days Jesus taketh Peter, James, and John his brother, and bringeth them up into an high mountain apart, And was transfigured before them: and his face did shine as the sun, and his raiment was white as the light. And, behold, there appeared unto them Moses and Elias talking with him. Then answered Peter, and said unto Jesus, Lord, it is good for us to be here: if thou wilt, let us make here three tabernacles; one for thee, and one for Moses, and one for Elias. While he yet spake, behold, a bright cloud overshadowed them: and behold a voice out of the cloud, which said, This is my beloved Son, in whom I am well pleased; hear ye him. And when the disciples heard it, they fell on their face, and were sore afraid. And Jesus came and touched them, and said, Arise, and be not afraid. And when they had lifted up their eyes, they saw no man, save Jesus only.

Although tradition has long held that Mount Tabor was the site of Jesus' transfiguration, most scholars now believe that in Christ's time a fortress city occupied Mount Tabor, making it an unlikely place for this event. Scholars thus point to Mount Hermon, pictured here during winter, as a more likely spot, since it is closer to Caesarea Philippi in the north, where Jesus and his disciples were staying.

Chapter Six

MIRACLES
OF
HEALING

The Nobleman's Son

JOHN 4:46–54

So Jesus came again into Cana of Galilee, where he made the water wine. And there was a certain nobleman, whose son was sick at Capernaum. When he heard that Jesus was come out of Judaea into Galilee, he went unto him, and besought him that he would come down, and heal his son: for he was at the point of death. Then said Jesus unto him, Except ye see signs and wonders, ye will not believe. The nobleman saith unto him, Sir, come down ere my child die. Jesus saith unto him, Go thy way; thy son liveth. And the man believed the word that Jesus had spoken unto him, and he went his way. And as he was now going down, his servants met him, and told him, saying, Thy son liveth. Then enquired he of them the hour when he began to amend. And they said unto him, Yesterday at the seventh hour the fever left him. So the father knew that it was at the same hour, in the which Jesus said unto him, Thy son liveth: and himself believed, and his whole house. This is again the second miracle that Jesus did, when he was come out of Judaea into Galilee.

Jesus spent a great deal of time in the village of Capernaum on the western shore of the Sea of Galilee, the ruins of which are pictured here. Capernaum was situated on an important trade route and was a major fishing site on the Sea of Galilee.

Peter's Mother-in-Law Is Cured

LUKE 4:38–44

And [Jesus] arose out of the synagogue, and entered into Simon's house. And Simon's wife's mother was taken with a great fever; and they besought him for her. And he stood over her, and rebuked the fever; and it left her: and immediately she arose and ministered unto them. Now when the sun was setting, all they that had any sick with divers diseases brought them unto him; and he laid his hands on every one of them, and healed them. And devils also came out of many, crying out, and saying, Thou art Christ the Son of God. And he rebuking them suffered them not to speak: for they knew that he was Christ. And when it was day, he departed and went into a desert place: and the people sought him, and came unto him, and stayed him, that he should not depart from them. And he said unto them, I must preach the kingdom of God to other cities also: for therefore am I sent. And he preached in the synagogues of Galilee.

The disciples Peter, Andrew, James, John, and Matthew were all called from the village of Capernaum. A church was eventually built over the ruins of the town, and it helps to mark the area where researchers think Peter's house was located. The photograph shows those ruins at Capernaum that archaeologists believe to be the house of the apostle Peter.

The Leper Cleansed

LUKE 5:12–15

And it came to pass, when [Jesus] was in a certain city, behold a man full of leprosy: who seeing Jesus fell on his face, and besought him, saying, Lord, if thou wilt, thou canst make me clean. And he put forth his hand, and touched him, saying, I will: be thou clean. And immediately the leprosy departed from him. And he charged him to tell no man: but go, and shew thyself to the priest, and offer for thy cleansing, according as Moses commanded, for a testimony unto them. But so much the more went there a fame abroad of him: and great multitudes came together to hear, and to be healed by him of their infirmities.

Although the Bible does not say which city Jesus was in when he healed the leper, it is believed the miracle took place in the vicinity of the Sea of Galilee. Perhaps the most prominent physical landmark around the Sea of Galilee is towering Mount Arbel, shown here. Located near the sea's western shore in the vicinity of ancient Magdala, home of Mary Magdalene, the mountain's sheer face can be easily picked out from most points around the lake. Below Mount Arbel lies a natural access route into the lake area and a route probably used by Jesus as he traveled back and forth to Cana and Nazareth.

Jesus Heals a Palsied Man

LUKE 5:17–25

And it came to pass on a certain day, as [Jesus] was teaching, that there were Pharisees and doctors of the law sitting by, which were come out of every town of Galilee, and Judaea, and Jerusalem: and the power of the Lord was present to heal them. And, behold, men brought in a bed a man which was taken with a palsy: and they sought means to bring him in, and to lay him before him. And when they could not find by what way they might bring him in because of the multitude, they went upon the housetop, and let him down through the tiling with his couch into the midst before Jesus. And when he saw their faith, he said unto him, Man, thy sins are forgiven thee. And the scribes and the Pharisees began to reason, saying, Who is this which speaketh blasphemies? Who can forgive sins, but God alone? But when Jesus perceived their thoughts, he answering said unto them, What reason ye in your hearts? Whether is easier, to say, Thy sins be forgiven thee; or to say, Rise up and walk? But that ye may know that the Son of man hath power upon earth to forgive sins, (he said unto the sick of the palsy,) I say unto thee, Arise, and take up thy couch, and go into thine house. And immediately he rose up before them, and took up that whereon he lay, and departed to his own house, glorifying God.

During New Testament times, the Pharisees were known for insisting that the people keep the "tradition of the elders," which were interpretations of the Scriptures by the Hebrew scribes. The Gospels sometimes refer to the Pharisees as lawyers because they were experts in the Mosaic Law. In this photograph, a modern-day scribe meticulously copies the Torah—the books of Moses.

Rise and Walk

JOHN 5:2–9

Now there is at Jerusalem by the sheep market a pool, which is called in the Hebrew tongue Bethesda, having five porches. In these lay a great multitude of impotent folk, of blind, halt, withered, waiting for the moving of the water. For an angel went down at a certain season into the pool, and troubled the water: whosoever then first after the troubling of the water stepped in was made whole of whatsoever disease he had. And a certain man was there, which had an infirmity thirty and eight years. When Jesus saw him lie, and knew that he had been now a long time in that case, he saith unto him, Wilt thou be made whole? The impotent man answered him, Sir, I have no man, when the water is troubled, to put me into the pool: but while I am coming, another steppeth down before me. Jesus saith unto him, Rise, take up thy bed, and walk. And immediately the man was made whole, and took up his bed, and walked.

Excavations in the Old City of Jerusalem have unearthed the pool of Bethesda, as shown here, located near the sheep gate, the gate farthest east on the northern wall. Large reservoirs of water were needed in the city, particularly for the temple sacrifices. Conduits were laid from large pools near Bethlehem and water was stored in several pools inside the city. Archaeologists have discovered two pools at the Bethesda site, measuring fifty-five and sixty-five feet long. The shorter pool has five arches over it with a porch beneath each arch, like the description in the Gosepl of John.

Stretch Forth Thy Hand

MARK 3:1–5

And [Jesus] entered again into the synagogue; and there was a man there which had a withered hand. And they watched him, whether he would heal him on the sabbath day; that they might accuse him. And he saith unto the man which had the withered hand, Stand forth. And he saith unto them, Is it lawful to do good on the sabbath days, or to do evil? to save life, or to kill? But they held their peace. And when he had looked round about on them with anger, being grieved for the hardness of their hearts, he saith unto the man, Stretch forth thine hand. And he stretched it out: and his hand was restored whole as the other.

When Jesus began his public ministry, he made it his habit to preach in the synagogues, most of which were built on the highest hill in the town, near water, and with an entrance toward the east, as was the temple in Jerusalem. The most important feature of the synagogue was the Torah Ark, which held copies of the sacred Scriptures. Worship on the Sabbath would include reading from the Torah and prayer. The synagogue at Capernaum, where Jesus healed the man with the withered hand, was built with the aid of the centurion whose servant Jesus also healed. The excavated ruins of the synagogue at Capernaum are shown at right.

MIRACLES OF HEALING 103

The Centurion's Servant

LUKE 7:1–10

Now when [Jesus] had ended all his sayings in the audience of the people, he entered into Capernaum. And a certain centurion's servant, who was dear unto him, was sick, and ready to die. And when he heard of Jesus, he sent unto him the elders of the Jews, beseeching him that he would come and heal his servant. . . . Then Jesus went with them. And when he was now not far from the house, the centurion sent friends to him, saying unto him, Lord, trouble not thyself: for I am not worthy that thou shouldest enter under my roof: Wherefore neither thought I myself worthy to come unto thee: but say in a word, and my servant shall be healed. For I also am a man set under authority, having under me soldiers, and I say unto one, Go, and he goeth; and to another, Come, and he cometh; and to my servant, Do this, and he doeth it. When Jesus heard these things, he marvelled at him, and turned him about, and said unto the people that followed him, I say unto you, I have not found so great faith, no, not in Israel. And they that were sent, returning to the house, found the servant whole that had been sick.

The Roman Empire controlled all of Europe and the Middle East during the time of Jesus. As well as building aqueducts, theaters, baths, and temples, the Romans built a vast network of roads across the empire. The carved stone pictured here is a Roman milestone at Capernaum in Galilee, probably close to the place where Jesus healed the centurion's servant. A centurion was a non-commissioned officer in charge of a "century" of one hundred men. Other centurions mentioned in the Bible include the centurion present at Jesus' crucifixion who declared him to be the Son of God and Cornelius, the first Gentile convert in Acts.

The Herd of Swine

MARK 5:2–13

And when he was come out of the ship, immediately there met him out of the tombs a man with an unclean spirit, who had his dwelling among the tombs; and no man could bind him, no, not with chains: because that he had been often bound with fetters and chains, and the chains had been plucked asunder by him, and the fetters broken in pieces: neither could any man tame him. And always, night and day, he was in the mountains, and in the tombs, crying, and cutting himself with stones. But when he saw Jesus afar off, he ran and worshipped him, And cried with a loud voice, and said, What have I to do with thee, Jesus, thou Son of the most high God? I adjure thee by God, that thou torment me not. For he said unto him, Come out of the man, thou unclean spirit. And he asked him, What is thy name? And he answered, saying, My name is Legion: for we are many. . . . Now there was there nigh unto the mountains a great herd of swine feeding. And all the devils besought him, saying, Send us into the swine, that we may enter into them. And forthwith Jesus gave them leave. And the unclean spirits went out, and entered into the swine: and the herd ran violently down a steep place into the sea, (they were about two thousand;) and were choked in the sea.

Pictured opposite are the ruins of a Byzantine monastery built on a hill in present-day Kursi—the area believed to correspond to the region of the Gadarenes and traditionally thought to be the site of the drowning of the swine.

Thy Faith Hath Made Thee Whole

MARK 5:25–34

And a certain woman, which had an issue of blood twelve years, and had suffered many things of many physicians, and had spent all that she had, and was nothing bettered, but rather grew worse, when she had heard of Jesus, came in the press behind, and touched his garment. For she said, If I may touch but his clothes, I shall be whole. And straightway the fountain of her blood was dried up; and she felt in her body that she was healed of that plague. And Jesus, immediately knowing in himself that virtue had gone out of him, turned him about in the press, and said, Who touched my clothes? And his disciples said unto him, Thou seest the multitude thronging thee, and sayest thou, Who touched me? And he looked round about to see her that had done this thing. But the woman fearing and trembling, knowing what was done in her, came and fell down before him, and told him all the truth. And he said unto her, Daughter, thy faith hath made thee whole; go in peace, and be whole of thy plague.

In Jesus' day, the Jews segregated the women in both the temple and the synagogues, but women accompanied Jesus and his disciples and provided money and sustenance on their journeys. He encouraged Mary and Martha to sit at his feet as his disciples and spoke lovingly to the Samaritan woman at the well. These Syrian women in present-day Damascus are wearing traditional dress.

The Phoenician Woman's Faith

MATTHEW 15:21–28

Then Jesus went thence, and departed into the coasts of Tyre and Sidon. And, behold, a woman of Canaan came out of the same coasts, and cried unto him, saying, Have mercy on me, O Lord, thou son of David; my daughter is grievously vexed with a devil. But he answered her not a word. And his disciples came and besought him, saying, Send her away; for she crieth after us. But he answered and said, I am not sent but unto the lost sheep of the house of Israel. Then came she and worshipped him, saying, Lord, help me. But he answered and said, It is not meet to take the children's bread, and to cast it to dogs. And she said, Truth, Lord: yet the dogs eat of the crumbs which fall from their masters' table. Then Jesus answered and said unto her, O woman, great is thy faith: be it unto thee even as thou wilt. And her daughter was made whole from that very hour.

The ancient city of Tyre was the principal seaport on the Phoenician coast (now Lebanon) and was a leader in commerce and trade. It consisted of two cities: a rocky coastal city on the mainland and a small island city. In New Testament times Tyre became a Roman colony, and its temple was built by Herod the Great. The Roman ruins shown here, of the Arch of Triumph in Tyre, would have been standing during the time of Jesus' ministry.

The Blind Shall See

MARK 8:22–26

And he cometh to Bethsaida; and they bring a blind man unto him, and besought him to touch him. And he took the blind man by the hand, and led him out of the town; and when he had spit on his eyes, and put his hands upon him, he asked him if he saw ought. And he looked up, and said, I see men as trees, walking. After that he put his hands again upon his eyes, and made him look up: and he was restored, and saw every man clearly. And he sent him away to his house, saying, Neither go into the town, nor tell it to any in the town.

There are two possible locations of the biblical Bethsaida where Jesus healed the blind man. One is on the western shore of the Sea of Galilee, near Capernaum, and the other is just east of the Jordan River where it runs into the lake. This photograph shows the latter site, on the mound of Et Tel where researchers believe they have unearthed old Bethsaida. Although the first settlement at Bethsaida was founded almost three thousand years ago, there are several houses and roads at this excavation site that date to the time of Jesus.

Casting a Devil from a Boy

MATTHEW 17:14–20

And when they were come to the multitude, there came to him a certain man, kneeling down to him, and saying, Lord, have mercy on my son: for he is lunatick, and sore vexed: for ofttimes he falleth into the fire, and oft into the water. And I brought him to thy disciples, and they could not cure him. Then Jesus answered and said . . . bring him hither to me. And Jesus rebuked the devil; and he departed out of him: and the child was cured from that very hour. Then came the disciples to Jesus apart, and said, Why could not we cast him out? And Jesus said unto them, Because of your unbelief: for verily I say unto you, If ye have faith as a grain of mustard seed, ye shall say unto this mountain, Remove hence to yonder place; and it shall remove; and nothing shall be impossible unto you.

Jesus healed the boy with a demon in the region of Caesarea Philippi, which was on the southern slopes of Mount Hermon in northern Israel. Numerous springs and waterfalls can be found in the area. In fact, one of the sources of the Jordan River lies in this region at Banias, in the Golan Heights of Israel, as shown here. The Greeks originally named the city Paneas after the god Pan, but the Romans changed the name to Caesarea Philippi in honor of Caesar and Philip the tetrarch. The present-day village of Banias is built on the same site, and excavations there have discovered the remains of the old city of Caesarea Philippi.

The Man Born Blind

JOHN 9:1–11

And as Jesus passed by, he saw a man which was blind from his birth. And his disciples asked him, saying, Master, who did sin, this man, or his parents, that he was born blind? Jesus answered, Neither hath this man sinned, nor his parents: but that the works of God should be made manifest in him. I must work the works of him that sent me, while it is day: the night cometh, when no man can work. As long as I am in the world, I am the light of the world. When he had thus spoken, he spat on the ground, and made clay of the spittle, and he anointed the eyes of the blind man with the clay, And said unto him, Go, wash in the pool of Siloam, (which is by interpretation, Sent.) He went his way therefore, and washed, and came seeing. The neighbours therefore, and they which before had seen him that he was blind, said, Is not this he that sat and begged? Some said, This is he: others said, He is like him: but he said, I am he. Therefore said they unto him, How were thine eyes opened? He answered and said, A man that is called Jesus made clay, and anointed mine eyes, and said unto me, Go to the pool of Siloam, and wash: and I went and washed, and I received sight.

The pool of Siloam has a history that goes back before the time of Christ. During King Hezekiah's reign, Hezekiah's Tunnel was built beneath the walls of Jerusalem in order to provide a water source for the city if surrounded by enemies. The tunnel was built to allow water from the Gihon Spring to flow into the city and to be emptied into a place called the pool of Siloam. Hezekiah's Tunnel and the Pool of Siloam are shown here, still in use today in the southeastern section of the Old City in Jerusalem.

The Ten Lepers

LUKE 17:11–19

And it came to pass, as he went to Jerusalem, that he passed through the midst of Samaria and Galilee. And as he entered into a certain village, there met him ten men that were lepers, which stood afar off: And they lifted up their voices, and said, Jesus, Master, have mercy on us. And when he saw them, he said unto them, Go shew yourselves unto the priests. And it came to pass, that, as they went, they were cleansed. And one of them, when he saw that he was healed, turned back, and with a loud voice glorified God, And fell down on his face at his feet, giving him thanks: and he was a Samaritan. And Jesus answering said, Were there not ten cleansed? but where are the nine? There are not found that returned to give glory to God, save this stranger. And he said unto him, Arise, go thy way: thy faith hath made thee whole.

The Samaritans in the time of Jesus were shunned by the Jews because of their mixed race. Jesus went out of his way to show compassion for the Samaritans, from the woman at the well, to the parable of the Good Samaritan, to the leper in the passage above. Mount Gerizim in Samaria was the place of Samaritan worship, where a temple was built to rival the one in Jerusalem. Its ruins are pictured here.

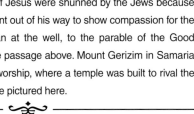

Blind Bartimaeus

MARK 10:46–52

As he went out of Jericho with his disciples and a great number of people, blind Bartimaeus, the son of Timaeus, sat by the highway side begging. And when he heard that it was Jesus of Nazareth, he began to cry out, and say, Jesus, thou son of David, have mercy on me. And many charged him that he should hold his peace: but he cried the more a great deal, Thou son of David, have mercy on me. And Jesus stood still, and commanded him to be called. And they call the blind man, saying unto him, Be of good comfort, rise; he calleth thee. And he, casting away his garment, rose, and came to Jesus. And Jesus answered and said unto him, What wilt thou that I should do unto thee? The blind man said unto him, Lord, that I might receive my sight. And Jesus said unto him, Go thy way; thy faith hath made thee whole. And immediately he received his sight, and followed Jesus in the way.

Situated at the foot of the Judean mountains about eight miles northwest of the Dead Sea, the ancient town of Jericho, pictured here, is an oasis in the midst of a very dry land. It is known as "the city of palms." The town was visited several times by Jesus, who healed blind Bartimaeus and called to Zaccheus there.

Compassion for an Enemy

LUKE 22:47–51

And while he yet spake, behold a multitude, and he that was called Judas, one of the twelve, went before them, and drew near unto Jesus to kiss him. But Jesus said unto him, Judas, betrayest thou the Son of man with a kiss? When they which were about him saw what would follow, they said unto him, Lord, shall we smite with the sword? And one of them smote the servant of the high priest, and cut off his right ear. And Jesus answered and said, Suffer ye thus far. And he touched his ear, and healed him.

Although the exact location of the Garden of Gethsemane is not known, there are several places traditionally revered as the site of Jesus' last night of prayer before his crucifixion. The garden lay on the Mount of Olives just east of Jerusalem, across the Kidron Valley and opposite the temple. Gethsemane means "olive press," perhaps indicating that it was situated in a grove that contained an olive press. The trees that grow on the Mount of Olives today are believed to be old enough to have witnessed Christ's agony in the Garden.

Chapter Seven

Miracles
of
Resurrection

The Only Son

LUKE 7:11–16

And it came to pass the day after, that he went into a city called Nain; and many of his disciples went with him, and much people. Now when he came nigh to the gate of the city, behold, there was a dead man carried out, the only son of his mother, and she was a widow: and much people of the city was with her. And when the Lord saw her, he had compassion on her, and said unto her, Weep not. And he came and touched the bier: and they that bare him stood still. And he said, Young man, I say unto thee, Arise. And he that was dead sat up, and began to speak. And he delivered him to his mother. And there came a fear on all: and they glorified God, saying, That a great prophet is risen up among us; and, That God hath visited his people.

It was part of Jewish custom to honor the dead with a funeral procession accompanied by the loud wails of relatives, and often professional mourners as well. The body was anointed with spices and carried on a bier. Jesus came upon such a procession in the town of Nain as he traveled from Capernaum. Nain, shown here, is reached from the west by a steep road that leads past rock tombs, and a short distance from the eastern road there is a small burial ground.

Jairus's Daughter

MARK 5:22-24, 35-42

And, behold, there cometh one of the rulers of the synagogue, Jairus by name; and when he saw him, he fell at his feet, And besought him greatly, saying, My little daughter lieth at the point of death: I pray thee, come and lay thy hands on her, that she may be healed; and she shall live. And Jesus went with him; and much people followed him, and thronged him. While he yet spake, there came from the ruler of the synagogue's house certain which said, Thy daughter is dead: why troublest thou the Master any further? As soon as Jesus heard the word that was spoken, he saith unto the ruler of the synagogue, Be not afraid, only believe. . . . he taketh the father and the mother of the damsel, and them that were with him, and entereth in where the damsel was lying. And he took the damsel by the hand, and said unto her, *Talitha cumi*; which is, being interpreted, Damsel, I say unto thee, arise. And straightway the damsel arose, and walked; for she was of the age of twelve years. And they were astonished with a great astonishment.

Galilee was the northernmost province in Palestine and covered more than a third of Palestine's territory. Its landscape consisted mostly of farmland and forests, and the Sea of Galilee, a major landmark in Jesus' ministry, was located in the heart of the province. Jesus performed eighteen of his thirty-three recorded miracles in the area of the Sea of Galilee, pictured above.

Lazarus

JOHN 11:1–3, 21–22, 32, 38–44

Now a certain man was sick, named Lazarus, of Bethany, the town of Mary and her sister Martha. . . . Therefore his sisters sent unto him, saying, Lord, behold, he whom thou lovest is sick. Then Martha, as soon as she heard that Jesus was coming, went and met him: but Mary sat still in the house. Then said Martha unto Jesus, Lord, if thou hadst been here, my brother had not died. But I know, that even now, whatsoever thou wilt ask of God, God will give it thee. Then when Mary was come where Jesus was, and saw him, she fell down at his feet, saying unto him, Lord, if thou hadst been here, my brother had not died. Jesus therefore again groaning in himself cometh to the grave. It was a cave, and a stone lay upon it. Jesus said, Take ye away the stone. Martha, the sister of him that was dead, saith unto him, Lord, by this time he stinketh: for he hath been dead four days. Jesus saith unto her, Said I not unto thee, that, if thou wouldest believe, thou shouldest see the glory of God? Then they took away the stone from the place where the dead was laid. And Jesus lifted up his eyes, and said, Father, I thank thee that thou hast heard me. And I knew that thou hearest me always: but because of the people which stand by I said it, that they may believe that thou hast sent me. And when he thus had spoken, he cried with a loud voice, Lazarus, come forth. And he that was dead came forth, bound hand and foot with graveclothes: and his face was bound about with a napkin. Jesus saith unto them, Loose him, and let him go.

The small town of Bethany is about two miles east of Jerusalem on the slopes of the Mount of Olives. It was the scene of several important events in the life of Jesus, and he was received as a guest numerous times in the home of Mary, Martha, and Lazarus. He spent at least one night in Bethany during the week before his crucifixion. The photo above shows the traditional site of Lazarus's tomb in the town of Bethany.

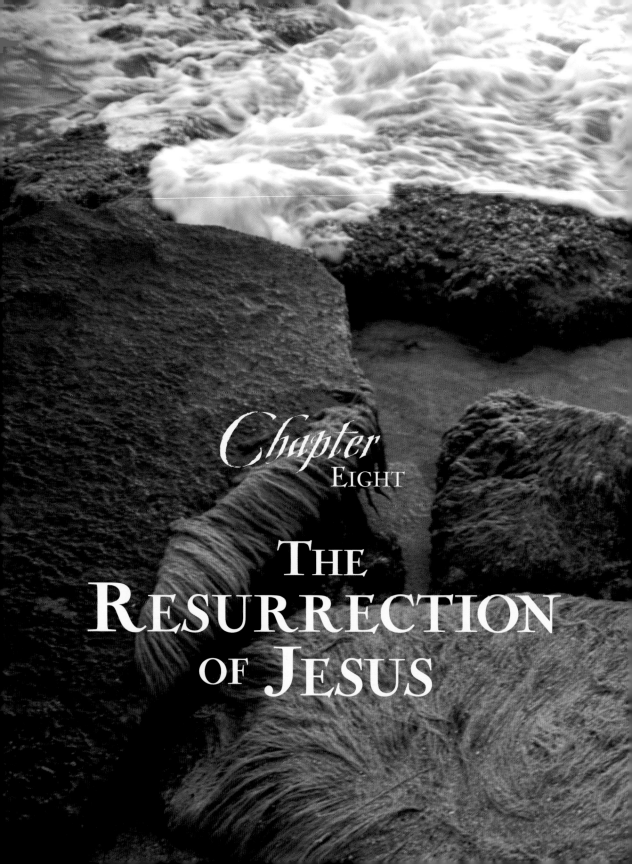

Chapter EIGHT

THE RESURRECTION OF JESUS

The Empty Tomb

LUKE 24:1–10

Now upon the first day of the week, very early in the morning, they came unto the sepulchre, bringing the spices which they had prepared, and certain others with them. And they found the stone rolled away from the sepulchre. And they entered in, and found not the body of the Lord Jesus. And it came to pass, as they were much perplexed thereabout, behold, two men stood by them in shining garments: And as they were afraid, and bowed down their faces to the earth, they said unto them, Why seek ye the living among the dead? He is not here, but is risen: remember how he spake unto you when he was yet in Galilee, Saying, The Son of man must be delivered into the hands of sinful men, and be crucified, and the third day rise again. And they remembered his words, And returned from the sepulchre, and told all these things unto the eleven, and to all the rest. It was Mary Magdalene and Joanna, and Mary the mother of James, and other women that were with them, which told these things unto the apostles.

In keeping with the burial practice of the day, Jesus' body was washed and dressed in linen sheets sprinkled with a mixture of spices and oil. Although many attempts have been made to discover the location of Jesus' tomb, questions still remain, even around those sites that seem most probable. The Church of the Holy Sepulchre is built over one site, while the other, the Garden Tomb, at right, is preserved intact just north of the city.

The Last Breakfast

JOHN 21:2–12

There were together Simon Peter, and Thomas called Didymus, and Nathanael of Cana in Galilee, and the sons of Zebedee, and two other of his disciples. Simon Peter saith unto them, I go a fishing. They say unto him, We also go with thee. They went forth, and entered into a ship immediately; and that night they caught nothing. But when the morning was now come, Jesus stood on the shore: but the disciples knew not that it was Jesus. Then Jesus saith unto them . . . Cast the net on the right side of the ship, and ye shall find. They cast therefore, and now they were not able to draw it for the multitude of fishes. Therefore that disciple whom Jesus loved saith unto Peter, It is the Lord. Now when Simon Peter heard that it was the Lord, he girt his fisher's coat unto him, (for he was naked,) and did cast himself into the sea. And the other disciples came in a little ship. . . . Jesus saith unto them, Bring of the fish which ye have now caught. Simon Peter went up, and drew the net to land full of great fishes, an hundred and fifty and three: and for all there were so many, yet was not the net broken. Jesus saith unto them, Come and dine. And none of the disciples durst ask him, Who art thou? knowing that it was the Lord.

The town of Tabgha on the Sea of Galilee's western shore is traditonally identified as the site of several episodes in Jesus' ministry. Its name means "seven springs," and Tabgha was a popular fishing spot because these springs produced warmer water that attracted fish. Jesus' calling of his disciples, saying he would make them "fishers of men," is thought to have taken place here, as well as the "last breakfast" with the disciples on the shores of the lake. The picture shown here is of a common site for prayer at Tabgha.

The Ascension

LUKE 24:44–52

And [Jesus] said unto them, These are the words which I spake unto you, while I was yet with you, that all things must be fulfilled, which were written in the law of Moses, and in the prophets, and in the psalms, concerning me. Then opened he their understanding, that they might understand the scriptures, And said unto them, Thus it is written, and thus it behoved Christ to suffer, and to rise from the dead the third day. . . . And ye are witnesses of these things. And, behold, I send the promise of my Father upon you: but tarry ye in the city of Jerusalem, until ye be endued with power from on high. And he led them out as far as to Bethany, and he lifted up his hands, and blessed them. And it came to pass, while he blessed them, he was parted from them, and carried up into heaven. And they worshipped him, and returned to Jerusalem with great joy.

The village of Bethany is situated on the slopes of the Mount of Olives, a north-to-south ridge of hills just east of Jerusalem. The Church of the Ascension, pictured here, stands on the spot believed by many to be the place where Jesus ascended into heaven. The city of Jerusalem can be seen in the background.

Chapter
NINE

MIRACLES
OF THE
DISCIPLES

Languages at Pentecost

ACTS 2:1–11

And when the day of Pentecost was fully come, they were all with one accord in one place. And suddenly there came a sound from heaven as of a rushing mighty wind, and it filled all the house where they were sitting. And there appeared unto them cloven tongues like as of fire, and it sat upon each of them. And they were all filled with the Holy Ghost, and began to speak with other tongues, as the Spirit gave them utterance. And there were dwelling at Jerusalem Jews, devout men, out of every nation under heaven. Now when this was noised abroad, the multitude came together, and were confounded, because that every man heard them speak in his own language. . . . Parthians, and Medes, and Elamites, and the dwellers in Mesopotamia, and in Judaea, and Cappadocia, in Pontus, and Asia, Phrygia, and Pamphylia, in Egypt, and in the parts of Libya about Cyrene, and strangers of Rome, Jews and proselytes, Cretes and Arabians, we do hear them speak in our tongues the wonderful works of God.

It is impossible to locate the exact site of the upper room where the miracle of tongues at Pentecost is believed to have occured. The picture shown here is of the room traditionally claimed to be the room of the Last Supper as well as the location of the gathering of the disciples for the miracle at Pentecost. It is called the Cenacle, located just outside the Zion Gate in the Old City of Jerusalem.

Peter and John at the Temple

ACTS 3:2–11

And a certain man lame from his mother's womb was carried, whom they laid daily at the gate of the temple which is called Beautiful, to ask alms of them that entered into the temple; Who seeing Peter and John about to go into the temple asked an alms. And Peter, fastening his eyes upon him with John, said, Look on us. And he gave heed unto them, expecting to receive something of them. Then Peter said, Silver and gold have I none; but such as I have give I thee: In the name of Jesus Christ of Nazareth rise up and walk. And he took him by the right hand, and lifted him up: and immediately his feet and ankle bones received strength. And he leaping up stood, and walked, and entered with them into the temple, walking, and leaping, and praising God. . . . And as the lame man which was healed held Peter and John, all the people ran together unto them in the porch that is called Solomon's, greatly wondering.

While little remains of Herod's temple in Jerusalem today, this archway leading to the Chain Gate on Jerusalem's Temple Mount gives us an image of what the Solomon's Porch area of the temple may have looked like.

Saul Receives Sight

ACTS 9:10–20

And there was a certain disciple at Damascus, named Ananias. . . . And the Lord said unto him, Arise, and go into the street which is called Straight, and enquire in the house of Judas for one called Saul, of Tarsus: for, behold, he prayeth, And hath seen in a vision a man named Ananias coming in, and putting his hand on him, that he might receive his sight. . . . But the Lord said unto him, Go thy way: for he is a chosen vessel unto me, to bear my name before the Gentiles, and kings, and the children of Israel: For I will shew him how great things he must suffer for my name's sake. And Ananias went his way, and entered into the house; and putting his hands on him said, Brother Saul, the Lord, even Jesus, that appeared unto thee in the way as thou camest, hath sent me, that thou mightest receive thy sight, and be filled with the Holy Ghost. And immediately there fell from his eyes as it had been scales: and he received sight forthwith, and arose, and was baptized. And when he had received meat, he was strengthened. Then was Saul certain days with the disciples which were at Damascus. And straightway he preached Christ in the synagogues, that he is the Son of God.

The city of Damascus is said to be the oldest continually inhabited city in the world. It was the capital of the Syrian nation at the time of Solomon, and was in turn occupied by the Assyrians and the Romans. It is the capital of modern-day Syria. The Damascus Gate in Jerusalem, pictured here, is the beginning of the road from that city that leads to Damascus, where Straight Street still exists today.

Peter Raises Dorcas

ACTS 9:36–42

Now there was at Joppa a certain disciple named Tabitha, which by interpretation is called Dorcas: this woman was full of good works and almsdeeds which she did. And it came to pass in those days, that she was sick, and died: whom when they had washed, they laid her in an upper chamber. And forasmuch as Lydda was nigh to Joppa, and the disciples had heard that Peter was there, they sent unto him two men, desiring him that he would not delay to come to them. Then Peter arose and went with them. When he was come, they brought him into the upper chamber: and all the widows stood by him weeping, and shewing the coats and garments which Dorcas made, while she was with them. But Peter put them all forth, and kneeled down, and prayed; and turning him to the body said, Tabitha, arise. And she opened her eyes: and when she saw Peter, she sat up. And he gave her his hand, and lifted her up, and when he had called the saints and widows, presented her alive. And it was known throughout all Joppa; and many believed in the Lord.

The ancient seaport of Joppa, on Israel's Mediteranean coast, is now called Jaffa. In the apostles' time Joppa was a walled city, and it supposedly received its name (which means *beautiful*) from the sunlight off the blue water reflected upon its buildings, as shown here.

Peter Escapes from Prison

ACTS 12:1–11

Now about that time Herod the king stretched forth his hands to vex certain of the church. And he killed James the brother of John with the sword. And . . . he proceeded further to take Peter also. . . . And when he had apprehended him, he put him in prison, and delivered him to four quaternions of soldiers to keep him; intending after Easter to bring him forth to the people. Peter therefore was kept in prison: but prayer was made without ceasing of the church unto God for him. And when Herod would have brought him forth, the same night Peter was sleeping between two soldiers, bound with two chains: and the keepers before the door kept the prison. And, behold, the angel of the Lord came upon him, and a light shined in the prison: and he smote Peter on the side, and raised him up, saying, Arise up quickly. And his chains fell off from his hands. And the angel said unto him, Gird thyself, and bind on thy sandals. And so he did. And he saith unto him, Cast thy garment about thee, and follow me. And he went out, and followed him. . . . When they were past the first and the second ward, they came unto the iron gate that leadeth unto the city; which opened to them of his own accord: and they went out, and passed on through one street; and forthwith the angel departed from him. And when Peter was come to himself, he said, Now I know of a surety, that the Lord hath sent his angel, and hath delivered me out of the hand of Herod.

This passage in the Armenian Quarter of the Old City in Jerusalem may be very like the streets through which Peter followed the angel in the night, as he was miraculously rescued from Herod's prison. The Old City of Jerusalem is now divided into four quarters: the Jewish Quarter, the Christian Quarter, the Muslim Quarter, and the Armenian Quarter. Much of the Armenian Quarter once comprised the palace of Herod the Great.

Paul and Barnabas

ACTS 14:8–15

And there sat a certain man at Lystra, impotent in his feet, being a cripple from his mother's womb, who never had walked: The same heard Paul speak: who stedfastly beholding him, and perceiving that he had faith to be healed, Said with a loud voice, Stand upright on thy feet. And he leaped and walked. And when the people saw what Paul had done, they lifted up their voices, saying in the speech of Lycaonia, The gods are come down to us in the likeness of men. . . . Which when the apostles, Barnabas and Paul, heard of, they rent their clothes, and ran in among the people, crying out, And saying, Sirs, why do ye these things? We also are men of like passions with you, and preach unto you that ye should turn from these vanities unto the living God, which made heaven, and earth, and the sea, and all things that are therein.

The New Testament city of Lystra was part of the Roman province of Lycaonia, located in what is today the region of Anatolia, Turkey. The home of Paul's companion Timothy, Lystra was built on a small hill about 150 feet above a plain that stretched from the cities of Iconium and Derbe, cities also visited by Paul on his missionary journey. Lake Beysehir Golu, shown here, is found in central Anatolia, Turkey.

Paul Heals the Sick

ACTS 19:11–17

And God wrought special miracles by the hands of Paul: So that from his body were brought unto the sick handkerchiefs or aprons, and the diseases departed from them, and the evil spirits went out of them. Then certain of the vagabond Jews, exorcists, took upon them to call over them which had evil spirits the name of the Lord Jesus, saying, We adjure you by Jesus whom Paul preacheth. And there were seven sons of one Sceva, a Jew, and chief of the priests, which did so. And the evil spirit answered and said, Jesus I know, and Paul I know; but who are ye? And the man in whom the evil spirit was leaped on them, and overcame them, and prevailed against them, so that they fled out of that house naked and wounded. And this was known to all the Jews and Greeks also dwelling at Ephesus; and fear fell on them all, and the name of the Lord Jesus was magnified.

Ephesus, located in what is now modern-day Turkey, was the largest city in the Roman province of Asia, and it was a prominent seaport on the coast of the Aegean Sea. Ephesus was central to the spread of early Christianity, and Paul lived in the city for almost three years, preaching the gospel and performing many miracles. It was also a center of pagan culture and religion, boasting a theater, baths, and the massive Temple of Diana, one of the Seven Wonders of the Ancient World. The photo opposite shows the Ephesian ruins of the Temple of Hadrian along Curetes Way.

Paul Raises Eutychus

ACTS 20:7-12

And upon the first day of the week, when the disciples came together to break bread, Paul preached unto them, ready to depart on the morrow; and continued his speech until midnight. And there were many lights in the upper chamber, where they were gathered together. And there sat in a window a certain young man named Eutychus, being fallen into a deep sleep: and as Paul was long preaching, he sunk down with sleep, and fell down from the third loft, and was taken up dead. And Paul went down, and fell on him, and embracing him said, Trouble not yourselves; for his life is in him. When he therefore was come up again, and had broken bread, and eaten, and talked a long while, even till break of day, so he departed. And they brought the young man alive, and were not a little comforted.

Located in what is now modern Turkey, Troas, though now in ruins, was visited by the apostle Paul three times and was the site of the miraculous resurrection of the boy Eutychus. In its day it was a large and important port city on the Aegean Sea. Troas, which literally means "the region around Troy," was situated about ten miles from the ruins of ancient Troy, the city memorialized in Homer's *Iliad*. Excavations at Troy, in the picture at right, continue today.

Geographic Sites

The miracles listed below are grouped by geographic location. The numbers on the map at the right correspond to the miracle. The page number of each miracle is shown in parentheses.

1 Paul raises Eutychus (156-157)
2 Paul heals the sick (154-155)
3 Paul heals the crippled man (152-153)
4 Miracles in Egypt:
   Aaron's rod turns into a serpent (24-25)
   The Nile turns to blood (26-27)
   All the firstborn in Egypt die (28-29)
5 God parts the Red Sea (32-33)
6 Miracles in the Sinai Wilderness:
   God provides a pillar of cloud and fire (30-31)
   God makes the bitter water sweet (36-37)
   God sends manna to the Israelites (38-39)
7 Miracles on Mount Sinai:
   God speaks to Moses in the burning bush (22-23)
   God gives Moses the Ten Commandments (40-41)
8 Ananias heals Paul's blindness (146-147)
9 Miracles in Zarephath:
   Elijah renews the widow's oil and meal (52-53)
   Elijah raises the widow's son from the dead (54-55)
10 Jesus heals the Phoenician woman's daughter of a demon (110-111)
11 Jesus is transfigured before his disciples (88-89)
12 Jesus casts a devil from a boy (114-115)
13 Miracles in Capernaum:
   Jesus heals the centurion's servant (104-105)

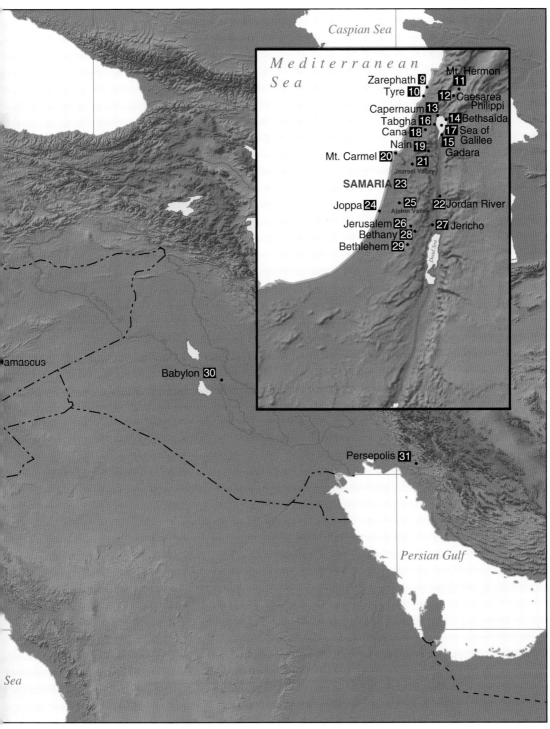

Caspian Sea

Mediterranean Sea

Zarephath **9**
Tyre **10**
Capernaum **13**
Tabgha **16**
Cana **18**
Nain **19**
Mt. Carmel **20**
21
Jezreel Valley
SAMARIA 23

Mt. Hermon
11
12 Caesarea Philippi
14 Bethsaida
17 Sea of
15 Galilee
Gadara

Joppa **24**
25
Ajalon Valley
Jerusalem **26**
Bethany **28**
Bethlehem **29**

22 Jordan River
27 Jericho
Dead Sea

amascus

Babylon **30**

Persepolis **31**

Persian Gulf

Sea

(continued from p. 4)

pp. 120-121 Alamy Images; pp. 122-123 Roberts Stock/R. Kord; pp. 124-125 Israel Images/Naftali Hilger; pp. 126-127 Israel Images/Hanan Isachar; pp. 128-129 Israel Images/Israel Talby; p. 131 Erich Lessing/Art Resource, NY; pp. 132-133 Israel Images/Israel Talby; p. 135 Israel Images/Hanan Isachar; pp. 136-137 Israel Images/Hanan Isachar; pp. 138-139 Israel Images/Hanan Isachar; pp. 140-141 Israel Images/Hanan Isachar; p. 143 Alamy Images; pp. 144-145 Israel Images; p. 147 Alamy Images; pp. 148-149 Israel Images/Hanan Isachar; p. 151 Israel Images/Garo Nalbandian; p. 152-153 Alamy Images; p. 155 Tony Stone/Robert Frerck (Getty Images); pp. 156-157 Taxi/Ulf Sjostedt (Getty Images).